•

THE

Pessimist's Journal

OF

Very, Very Bad Days

•

Compiled by Jess Brallier and
Richard P. McDonough

Designed by Janis Owens

Little, Brown and Company
Boston • Toronto • London

to Sally
—JMB

à toi et vous
—RPM

First Edition

ISBN 0-316-10600-3

10   9   8   7   6   5   4   3   2

BP

Published simultaneously in Canada
by Little, Brown & Company (Canada) Limited

Printed in the United States of America

The optimist proclaims that we live
in the best of all possible worlds, the
pessimist fears this is true.
— James Branch Cabell

Pessimism is as American as apple
pie–frozen apple pie with a slice of
processed cheese.
— George F. Will

CODE KEY

❷ Unable to confirm exact date. None of the parties
involved admits to anything regarding this matter.

🐟 Unwilling to confirm exact date. Further
research into this matter is simply too depressing.

☢ Unwilling to confirm the exact date on this.
What's the use? There's an election coming up, it's been
raining acid rain for three straight days, there's radon
in the basement, there's medical waste on the beach,
taxes are going up, the Supreme Court's in session, the
new TV season is beginning, and the power plant's
been making funny noises all morning.

—The Pessimist
February, 1989

January

•

I thought what was good for the
country was good for General
Motors, and vice versa.
— Charles E. Wilson,
    President of General Motors,
    upon his appointment as
    Secretary of Defense

•

JANUARY

1 This is going to be one awful year, believe me.

2 Tipper Gore escalates her battle against pornographic rock 'n' roll lyrics. (1988)

3 In 1920 the Boston Red Sox trade away Babe Ruth (he's only got 665 home runs left in him) and 53 years later George Steinbrenner gains controlling interest in the New York Yankees.

4 First tufted plastic carpeting goes on sale. (1953)

5 Marshmallow is invented. (1927) ❧

6 In order to "protect American interests," United States Marines are sent to Nicaragua. (1927)

7 Birth of Millard Fillmore. (1800)

8 General Andrew Jackson's troops inflict over 2,000 casualties in a crushing defeat of the British forces at the Battle of New Orleans . . . two weeks after a treaty ended the war. (1815)

9 In 1873 Reverend Henry Ward Beecher is charged with adultery, escapes the suit on a legal technicality, and thereafter draws larger crowds than ever—particularly when preaching on sin; then in 1913 Richard Nixon is born.

10 The world's first correspondence course is offered. (1840)

11 America's first life insurance company is founded: The Corporation for Relief of Poor and Distressed Widows and Children of Presbyterian Ministers. (1759)

12 Princess Anne announces, "I don't actually like children." (1986)

13 Arizona Governor Evan Mecham rescinds the order making Martin Luther King's birthday a holiday. (1987)

JANUARY

14 Donna Griffiths of Pershore, England, starts sneezing and she'll not stop for another 978 days. (1981)

15 Jim Garry ends his career with an ERA of 63.00, all the result of his only major league appearance: one inning pitched, 5 hits, 4 walks, 7 runs . . . and he took the loss. (1917)

16 Prohibition goes into effect. (1920)

17 Tony Orlando records "Tie a Yellow Ribbon 'Round the Old Oak Tree." (1975) ❷

18 In 1934 Muzak is heard for the first time . . . in the lobby and restaurant of a hotel in Cleveland.

19 Gene Shalit decides to grow a mustache. (1968) ☙

JANUARY

20 The Rev. Billy Graham gives thanks that "in Thy sovereignty Thou hast permitted Richard Nixon to lead us at this momentous hour of our history." (Inauguration Day, 1969)

21 TV's first cooking demonstration—Marcel Boulestin whips up an omelette in 1937.

22 Jane "Barbarella" Fonda's exercise video is on the top of the sales charts. (1985)

23 Australia currently in possession of America's Cup. (1983)

24 Secretary of the Interior James Watt declares, "We have every kind of mixture you can have. I have a black, I have a woman, two Jews and a cripple." (1983) ❷

25 A press release from Rajneesh headquarters announces that Indian religious leader Bhagwan Rajneesh must alter his name, having discovered that Bhagwan means genitals. (1989)

26 In 1978 Tammy Bakker recalls an earlier moment with Jim: "When I got in from bowling that night, Jim Bakker, the hall monitor, told me it wasn't nice for me to go out with ten boys. He said it would ruin my reputation." ❷

27 George Bush nominates John Tower for Secretary of Defense. (1989)

28 Jim "The Mouth" Purol simultaneously smokes 140 cigarettes for five minutes. (1983)

29 The White House confirms that a Bible inscribed by President Reagan was delivered to Iranian leaders. (1987)

30 First laugh track used in television. (1952) ❷

31 Jon Clark, adopted son of jazz musician Mr. Billy Timpton, is told by the undertaker that his father was a woman. "He'll always be Dad," Clark said. (1989)

February

•

If you can find something to laugh at
these days, you're not paying attention.
— Groucho Marx

•

FEBRUARY

1 There will be groundhog stories to contend with all day.

2 Ida Stern, age 91, and her husband, Simon Stern, age 97, divorce. (1984)

3 "Journalist" Geraldo Rivera did yesterday's show, naked, from a nudist camp. (1989)

4 Birth of James Danforth Quayle. (1947)

5 Under the cover of darkness, the Colts sneak out of Baltimore and head for Indianapolis. (1987) ☣

6 1943: birth of Fabian.

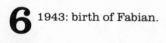

FEBRUARY

7 Ed Koch is still New York City's mayor. (1989)

8 Alabama Governor George Wallace announces he'll run for President keeping peace in the streets with "30,000 troops and two-foot-long bayonets." (1968)

9 "I have in my hand a list of 205 . . . " says Senator McCarthy in Wheeling, West Virginia. (1950)

10 A St. Louis couple names their newborn son Rambo. (1985)

11 Police rescue a naked Winona, Minnesota, couple from a collapsible sofa bed after they had folded it shut around themselves in an attempt to copy a stunt seen on the "stupid human tricks" segment of "Late Night with David Letterman." (1989)

12 The first Susan B. Anthony silver dollar is struck at the U.S. Mint in Philadelphia. (1974)

13 Oral Roberts raises $8 million and God doesn't call him home. (1987) ☉

14 Studebaker Automobiles incorporated. (1911)

15 That smiling "have-a-nice-day" face is back according to <u>The New York Times</u>. (1989)

16 John Tower promises the nation in 1989 that he will stop drinking, but only if the Senate will let him be in charge of the machinery of war.

17 The first sardine is canned. (1876)

18 Pete Rozelle starts numbering the Super Bowls with roman numerals. (MCMLXVII) ♣

19 The Vice President of the United States, Aaron Burr, is arrested for organizing an expedition to invade Mexico. (1807)

20 In 1979 Roy Cohn celebrates his 52nd birthday at Studio 54 with friend and client Steve Rubell.

21 The United States establishes the Federal Post Office System. (1792)

22 The phrase "the check is in the mail" is coined. (1792)

23 The national debt is $2,726,869,809,433.00. That's $2.7 trillion, or $41,946 per family. (1989)

24 The national debt is greater today than it was yesterday. (1989)

25 Robert Goulet forgets some of the words to "The Star-Spangled Banner" while singing at the Liston-Ali match. (1964)

26 Six thousand shoes found in Imelda Marcos's closet. (1986)

27 As predicted by the stars, White House Chief of Staff Donald Regan is fired. (1987)

28 This is usually the last day of February. Nothing much happens except that where it is cold it will be unbearable and where it snows there will be more snow than anyone can deal with; while in places where it is warm, people from places where it is cold will become overexposed to the sun and be in pain, if not in mortal danger.

29 And just in case you haven't had enough of February, here's a quadrennial extra during which the popular media will be packed with leap year baby stories.

March

•

The second half of the 20th century is a complete flop.

— Isaac Bashevis Singer

•

MARCH

1 Marc Christian (Rock Hudson's $21 million lover) tells a People interviewer in 1989 that he is "more and more . . . attracted to the idea of a heterosexual relationship."

2 Ray Kroc begins the franchising of McDonald's. (1955)

3 President Hoover signs the act that makes "The Star-Spangled Banner" the national anthem. (1931)

4 Time Inc. launches People magazine. (1974)

5 When Los Angeles police at last locate a Mazda sedan with unpaid parking violations totaling $11,598, it's legally parked. (1988)

6 Birth of Ed McMahon. (1923)

7 Commenting on the Symbionese Liberation Army's ransom demand of free food for the poor, California Governor Ronald Reagan complains, "It's just too bad we can't have an epidemic of botulism." (1974)

8 Clarence Birdseye's frozen foods first appear on the shelves of America's markets. (1930)

9 Ferdinand Marcos and Imelda meet. (1947) ✎

10 Birth of actor Robert Wagner. (1930)

11 An aide to Arizona Governor Evan Mecham testifies that his boss's activities are divinely inspired. (1987)

12 Jimmy Swaggart declares: "Pornography—those books with pictures and dirty movies—you would be shocked and surprised at the number of Christians who are 'hooked' on these things." (1986) ✎

13 Shrapnel-shaped "Rambo" candy is introduced. (1985) ❷

14 Burt Reynolds poses nude in <u>Cosmopolitan</u>. (1972)

15 Shortly after 11 A.M., and only after Brutus went to get him, Julius Caesar enters the newly built Senate. (44 BC)

16 Birth of Jerry Lewis. (1926)

17 An unidentified upstate New York woman is the first to wear pea green polyester stretch pants to a shopping mall. (1954) ✎

18 John and Cristina DeLorean become born-again Christians. (1983) ✎

19 For the first time, the Academy Awards ceremonies are nationally televised. (1953)

20 This morning—like every other morning of his adult life—Henry Ford II looked in his mirror and said, "I am King . . . and the King can do no wrong!" (1965)

21 U.S. Marines land in Honduras to protect American lives and capital investments in banana plantations from "things like revolution." (1907)

MARCH

22 President Truman signs Executive Order #9835, calling for a loyalty investigation of all Federal employees. (1947)

23 Yesterday the President told the Attorney General, "I don't give a shit what happens. I want you all to stonewall it, let them plead the 5th Amendment, cover up or anything else. . . ." (1973)

24 It's been two days since the sanitation barge <u>Mobro</u> departed Long Island in search of a place to dump New York's garbage. (1987)

25 First aluminum siding sales agreement signed. (1951) 🦅

26 Barbara Walters makes a commitment to pursue a career in TV journalism/broadcasting. (1957) ☢

27 First "Baby on Board" sign appears. (1986)

28 Only 48 more hours until Robin Leach's "Lifestyles of the Rich and Famous" premieres. (1984)

29 The United States awards more medals for service during the Grenada invasion than there were troops involved. (1984)

30 Al Haig announces, "As of now, I'm in control here." (1981)

31 Cordis Corporation admits to having sold 2,200 defective heart pacemakers. (1989)

April

•

God himself could not sink this ship.
— Deckhand, the <u>Titanic</u>

I don't know, sir, but I don't suppose
it's much.
— <u>Titanic</u> steward to a passenger
asking why the ship had stopped

•

APRIL

1 Birth of Ali McGraw (1939) and the first day in the month when the Boston Red Sox again take to the field.

2 Yesterday, the "unsinkable" <u>Titanic</u> completed and passed her trials. (1912)

3 Jesse James killed by his gang for the reward money. (1882)

4 Pat Robertson first smiles. (1931) ♟

5 DC Comics revises the character of Superman to make him "more open about his feelings . . . and more upwardly mobile." (1986) ✈

6 Saying they attract "the wrong element," Secretary of the Interior James Watt bans The Beach Boys from the Washington Mall Fourth of July Celebration and he instead promises "the military people, with their patriotism, and Wayne Newton." (1983)

7 Nancy Reagan finds out what James Watt said yesterday. (1983)

8 The Beach Boys are now saddled with the public knowledge that they are Nancy Reagan's favorite band. (1983)

9 Halley's Comet due tomorrow!!! (1986)

10 The "unsinkable" <u>Titanic</u> narrowly escapes collision with the American liner <u>New York</u> as she departs Southampton dock. (1912)

11 President Nixon says of the Watergate break-in, "I condemn any attempt to cover up this case, no matter who is involved." (1973)

12 Former White House spokesperson Larry Speakes admits he made up quotes for President Reagan because the President "had almost nothing to say." (1988)

13 The Houston Zoo's curator admits that the coral snake on display is made of rubber, but that's "because the real ones keep dying." (1984) ✿

14 The "unsinkable" <u>Titanic</u> strikes an iceberg at 11:40 P.M. (1912)

15 Income Tax is due, Abraham Lincoln dies (1865), and the "unsinkable" <u>Titanic</u> sinks. (1912)

16 Federal agents get ready for tomorrow's arrest of 16 Wall Street brokers and senior partners on charges of distributing cocaine in return for cash, stock, and customer information. (1987)

17 Presidential News Secretary Ron Ziegler declares all previous statements regarding the Watergate mess as "inoperative." (1973)

18 The "Los Angeles" before Dodgers in the newspaper this morning is not an error. (1958)

APRIL

19 Duke Antonio Fernando, who never drank because a fortune-teller warned that alcohol would kill him, catches fire and burns to death after rubbing his sore muscles with alcohol. (1729)

20 Paul Revere arrives home to Boston after walking all the way from yesterday's Milestone Battle in Lexington where his horse was commandeered into British army service. (1775)

21 The last passenger pigeon buys the farm. (1914)❷

22 The Army-McCarthy hearings open and the Senator from Wisconsin utters "point of order" for the first of many times. (1954)

23 Coca-Cola announces it's scrapping its 99-year-old recipe for the world's best-selling soft drink. (1985)

24 Donald Regan inks a $1 million contract for his memoirs. (1987)

25 Shirley MacLaine was born yesterday for the ___th (reader is free to insert whatever number he or she wishes) time. (1934)

26 The Philippines government confirms that Ferdinand and Imelda made off with $10 billion from the country's treasury. (1986)

27 The first Department of Agriculture tobacco subsidy is paid. (1933) ❷

28 After 16 games George Steinbrenner fires Yankee Manager Yogi Berra and hires Billy Martin. (1985)

29 Mrs. Miriam Hargrave crashes through a set of red lights and thus fails her driving test for the 39th time. She vows to try again on August 3. (1970)

30 Clarence Duffy resigned yesterday from the Dubuque, Iowa, Human Rights Commission after blaming slow mail delivery on "all those stupid broads we have working in the Post Office now." (1984)

May

•

. . . Vice President [Bush] attended several
meetings on the Iran initiative, but none
of the participants could re-call his views.
— Final report of the
Iran-Contra Committee

•

1 Tomorrow's <u>Newsweek</u> cover reads, "Special Report: HITLER'S SECRET DIARIES." (1984)

2 Confederate General "Stonewall" Jackson is fatally wounded by his own troops. (1863)

3 White House scheduling, we learn, is heavily dependent on the advice of Nancy Reagan's astrologer. (1988)

4 Jockey Willie Shoemaker misjudges the finish line and stands in his stirrups while Iron Liege passes him to win the 1957 Kentucky Derby.

5 John T. Scopes, a biology teacher in Dayton, Tennessee, is arrested for teaching the theory of evolution. (1925)

6 Donna Rice tells <u>The Los Angeles Times</u>, "I hate womanizers." (1987)

7 Jim Bakker talks to God, "Lord, if You want me to have that house in California you can help me make the payments just as you can help me make the payments on this one in Charlotte." (1978) ❓

8 Jean Baptiste Lully inadvertently stabs himself in the foot with his baton during a concert and is mortally wounded. (1687) ♣

9 <u>Faux</u> replaces <u>phoney</u> as the adjective of choice. (1986)

10 R. Leonard Vance, an official of the Occupational Safety and Health Administration, tells congressional investigators he's unable to supply certain crucial documents because his dog threw up on them. (1985) ❧

11 First computerized telephone sales call made to someone just settled into the bathtub. (1975) ❷

12 The first Harlequin romance is published. (1949)

13 Bebe Rebozzo and Richard Nixon still best of friends (1969), Rocco Riccobonno and Jessica Hahn are not. (1989)

MAY

14 1,400 fans travel from as far away as Japan and Australia to spend the weekend in Schaumburg, Illinois, attending the first annual Barry Manilow International Convention. (1983) ✤

15 Within an hour of George Wallace being shot, Charles Colson reportedly orders E. Howard Hunt to break into Arthur Bremer's apartment and plant Black Panther party newspapers and Angela Davis literature. (1972)

16 The <u>Titanic</u>'s sister ship, the <u>Olympic</u>, rams and sinks the lightship <u>Nantucket</u>. (1934)

17 Charles Colson gets reduced sentence and religion. (1974) ✤

18 Fidel Castro's hopes for a film career dashed as he is cast only as an extra in <u>Bathing Beauty</u>. (1944)

19 <u>Ishtar</u> premieres. (1987)

MAY

20 Birth of Cher. (1946)

21 The first Democractic Party National Convention opens in Baltimore. (1832)

22 Willard Scott decides to be a TV weather forecaster. (1959) ❧

23 President Reagan awards Frank Sinatra the American Medal of Freedom. (1985)

24 Vanna White announced yesterday that she will share all with us by penning her memoirs. Her publisher pays her $750,000. (1987)

25 First auto-repair shop opens. (1899)

26 Pittsburgh Pirate Harvey Haddix pitches 12 perfect innings of baseball, then loses in the 13th on one hit. (1959)

27 Achsah Young of Massachusetts is hanged as a witch; which explains why no one's ever used that name again. (1647)

28 As grieving family, friends, and classic car collectors look on, a 1964 Ferrari and its deceased owner—propped up behind the steering wheel—are laid to rest. (1977) ❷

29 Edward W. Bok, editor of <u>The Ladies' Home Journal</u>, fires 15 women after he catches them dancing the Turkey Trot during their lunch period. (1912)

30 A car driven by a Massachusetts man collides with a bicycle, thus marking the nation's first automobile accident. (1896)

31 The "unsinkable" <u>Titanic</u> is launched from the Belfast shipyards of Harland & Wolff. (1911)

June

•

No matter how cynical I get, I just can't keep up.

— Lily Tomlin

•

JUNE

1 Baron de Zuylen's Peugeot becomes the world's first stolen car. (1896)

2 New York threatens George Willig with a $250,000 damage suit for climbing the face of the World Trade Tower. (1977)

3 The New York City Police Department puts its first meter maids on staff. (1960)

4 Tris Speaker notes, "Babe Ruth made a mistake when he gave up pitching. Working once a week he might have lasted a long time and become a star." (1921) ✜

5 Robert Vesco remains at large. (1979)

6 Martha Crawford von Auersperg ("Sunny") and Claus von Bulow marry. (1966)

JUNE

7 Versailles becomes venue for Eugen Weidman's fleeting moment of fame as he becomes France's last criminal to be guillotined in public. (1939)

8 The Los Angeles City Council outlaws the wearing of zoot suits. (1943)

9 Gatling's Funeral Home in Chicago opens a drive-thru service so grieving friends, family, and former lovers might view the deceased—via a video screen—and pay their respects without going to the trouble of parking their cars. (1987) ❷

10 Cincinnati's Joe Nuxhall, in his first career start, pitches .2 innings and gives up five runs for an ERA of 67.5. Joe's next starting assignment comes eight years later. (1944)

11 The United States bans <u>Lady Chatterly's Lover</u>. (1959)

12 Senator Huey Long of Louisiana begins a 15 1/2 hour, 150,000 word filibuster—including recipes—which fills 100 pages of the <u>Congressional Record</u>, costing taxpayers additional printing costs of $5,000. (1935)

13 A Japanese naval academy student formulates an answer to a now standard tactical exercise question that asks how the student would plan and initiate a surprise attack on Pearl Harbor. (1931)

14 The Boston Red Sox commit 24 errors in a game with St. Louis. (1876)

15 After weeks of fighting that ultimately result in scores of dead penguins, the British at last overcome Argentina in the Falkland Islands war. (1982)

16 Tomorrow the first Republican Party National Convention will open. (1836)

17 Former CIA man Gordon Liddy, in the company of others, bungles a simple second-story job. (1972)

18 Ludmilla Sirogof's husband sues her for bankrupting him by charging for sex at the rate of $200 per session throughout their 28 years of marriage. (1984) ❷

19 Birth of Wallis Warfield Simpson; and her attending physician does not say, "She's fit for a king." (1895)

20 A CIA-backed right-wing coup overthrows the elected government of Guatemala, which, by chance, had just nationalized the property of the United Fruit Company. (1954)

21 Ed Meese applies to law school. (1949)

22 Cleveland's Cuyahoga River catches fire this date in 1969, just as it had in 1952, and for six days in 1936.

23 Without consulting Him or Her, the phrase "under God" was added to the pledge of allegiance nine days ago. (1954)

24 The New York garbage barge <u>Mobro</u> is still out there somewhere. (1987)

25 General George Custer gets his hair cut short prior to his engagement today at Bull Run. (1876)

26 A physician is disciplined by the New York Board of Regents for performing bladder and prostate operations after becoming blind. (1984) ☣

27 Secretary of State Henry Kissinger comments on his efforts to "destabilize" the democratically elected government of Chile, "I don't see why we need to stand by and watch a country go communist due to the irresponsibility of its own people." (1970)

28 In Sarajevo, Archduke Franz Ferdinand goes out for a breath of fresh air. (1914)

29 Ivy Lee sets himself up as the first "public relations" consultant; his first clients include a circus, some bankers, and politicians. (1903) ☣

30 Jimmy Hoffa is rumored to have become part of a highway somewhere in America. (1975) ❷

July

•

I should like to interview Monsieur
Marat [Jean Paul Marat, French rev-
olutionary] so as to put him into a
condition that will serve France well.
— Marie Anne Charlotte Corday,
     on July 13, 1793, just prior to her
     plunging a knife into Marat's heart
     as he was bathing

•

JULY

1 In 1948, New York's five-cent subway fare comes to an end.

2 Yesterday WNBV-TV ran the world's first television commercial. (1941)

3 Confederate General George S. Pickett decides that the thing to do is charge across a wheat field outside of Gettysburg. (1863)

4 Hundreds of Elvis Presley imitators perform in the official celebration of the nation's unveiling of the refurbished Statue of Liberty. (1986)

JULY

5 SPAM celebrates its 50th anniversary. (1987)

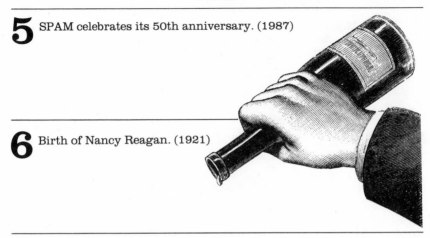

6 Birth of Nancy Reagan. (1921)

7 Despite his conviction for taking $250,000, Jimmy Hoffa is re-elected to a five-year term as Teamsters' President. (1965)

8 1835: The Liberty Bell cracks.

9 Birth of Barbara Cartland. (1901)

10 Zachary Taylor died last night of cholera morbus, after having eaten spoiled cherries, and Millard Fillmore is now President. (1850)

JULY

11 Stu Miller, while pitching at San Francisco's Candlestick Park in the All-Star game, is blown off the mound by a gust of wind. (1961)

12 "Awesome" creeps into the language. (1985)

13 One day in the late 19th century, and it might as well have been this one, Alfred Nobel invented dynamite.

14 The Republican Convention opens and, passing over Harold Stassen, nominates Ronald Reagan for the Presidency. (1980)

15 The fashion world unleashes the Nehru jacket. (1967) ✎

16 The first parking meter goes into service. (1935)

17 Disneyland opens. (1955)

18 The Democratic Convention opens in Atlanta and in all the confusion Michael Dukakis ends up being nominated for President. (1988)

JULY

19 Pilot Douglas "Wrongway" Corrigan takes off for Los Angeles . . . and lands in Dublin. (1938)

20 George Donner's party takes a shortcut over the Sierras. (1846)

21 Yesterday the Apollo Astronauts left Richard Nixon's signature on the moon. (1969)

22 Seeing that his favorite actress, Myrna Loy, is starring in <u>Manhattan Melodrama</u>, John Dillinger asks his girlfriend out to the movies. She puts on something red, and they head for the Biograph. (1934)

23 1988: Testimony from the Iran-Contra hearings has yet to determine who baked the cake.

24 In São Paulo, Brazil, 26 killer bees from Africa escape the laboratory of Warrick Kerr and begin interbreeding within minutes. (1951)

25 Jerry Hall points out that "if I weren't so beautiful maybe I'd have more character." (1978)

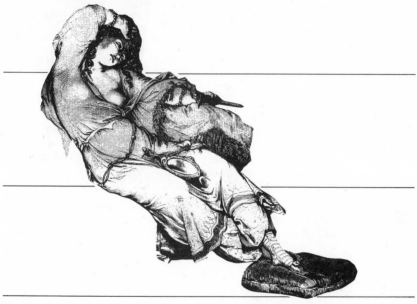

26 Imelda Marcos denies her extravagant spending splurges, claiming instead that she's too busy to shop because she's always "thinking about electrical power, education, roads, bridges, and transportation." (1985)

27 Campaigner Ronald Reagan tells the crowd in Youngstown that trees pollute the air. (1980)

28 Today Leo Buscaglia has already considered, is now contemplating, or will soon think about hugging somebody. (1989)

29 The Japanese invent underwear to be worn six days straight—"the wearer rotates it 120-degrees each day, and then wears it inside out for another three." (1984)

30 Yesterday, after two days of testimony at the Iran-Contra hearings, the Attorney General of the United States, Edwin Meese, had said "I don't recall," or words quite similar, 187 times. (1987)

31 On this July day in 2025 a time capsule somewhere in Nebraska will be opened and a blue leisure suit with stitched flowers and a bolt of virgin polyester will be found inside.

August

•

For the second time in our history, a British Prime Minister has returned from Germany bringing peace with honor. I believe it is peace for our time. Go home and get a nice quiet sleep.
—Neville Chamberlain, 1938

This war, like the next war, is a war to end war.
—David Lloyd George, 1940

•

1 The South Carolina Highway Department paints a yellow stripe across a dead cat lying in the road. (1987) ❷

2 Wonder Bread introduced. (1930)

3 On her 40th attempt, Mrs. Miriam Hargrave passes her driving test; but having spent $720 on 212 driving lessons, she can no longer afford a car. (1970)

4 At the Toronto Blue Jays ballpark, a sea gull is killed when hit with a ball thrown by Yankee Dave Winfield, and Canadian police arrest the outfielder for cruelty to animals. (1983)

5 At the intersection of Cleveland's Euclid and East 105th, the world's first traffic signal lights are installed. (1914)

6 The Richmond (Virginia) Chamber of Commerce petitions to re-name Main Street because of the bad image created by the Sinclair Lewis novel. (1921)

7 280,000 Japanese in Brazil, disbelieving that Japan lost the war, dispatch a representative to the mother country to disprove the rumors. (1951)

8 "Old-Fashioned Microwaveable Turkey and Stuffing" is introduced. (1988) ❦

9 Pep, the dog that killed Pennsylvania Governor Pinchot's cat, languishes in his cell at the state penitentiary where he's been sentenced to life imprisonment. (1924)

AUGUST

10 First scratch and sniff ad. (1966)

11 Young Richard Nixon sharpens his skills as a barker for a carnival game at the Slippery Gulch Rodeo. (1929)

12 A week ago today Congress enacted the first income tax law. (1861)

13 Radio station KLUE in Longview, Texas, holds a bonfire to immolate Beatles records and pictures in retaliation for a blasphemous statement by John Lennon. (1966)

14 Radio station KLUE's transmitter struck by lightning. (1966)

15 Opening (in New Orleans) of the Republican Convention which nominates James Danforth Quayle for the Vice Presidency. (1988)

AUGUST

16 In a memo to Ehrlichman, White House counsel John Dean submits a list of "enemies" to "screw," and at the top of the Priority List is Paul Newman. (1971)

17 Alexander Woollcott's ashes arrive at Hamilton College, 67-cents postage due. (1934)

18 Zoning approved for Levittown. (1947)

19 A CIA-initiated coup overthrows Iran's popularly elected government soon after it had nationalized the country's oil industry. (1953)

20 "When I look at my children," Lillian Carter notes, "I often wish I had remained a virgin." (1985) ☘

21 Twelve women are sent from England to Virginia to be sold as wives; the price is 120 pounds of tobacco each, or approximately one pound of tobacco for one pound of woman. (1621)

22 The National Board of Censorship forces the movie producers of Hawthorne's <u>The Scarlet Letter</u> to change a few things; for one, Hester has to get married. (1926)

AUGUST

23 TWA begins providing passengers with recipes for its in-flight meals. (1984) ☻

24 Elena Glinskaya goes into labor. The boy she gives birth to the next day, Ivan (the Terrible), will at age eight fatally poison her. (1540)

25 Although he was warned just two months earlier for driving at 95 mph in a 55 mph zone, California awards 104-year-old Roy Rawlins a driver's license valid for another four years. (1974)

26 The 1968 Democratic Convention, hosted by Mayor Richard J. Daley and his police, opens.

27 Norman Mailer declares that "women should be kept in cages." (1970) ☙

28 It is now known that until the age of ten, Michael Reagan thought that the family's black cook was his mother. (1988)

29 Shelley Winters' autobiography is published and the whole world gets to read about her sex life. (1980)

30 Idi Amin remains at large. (1989)

31 The National Enquirer reports that Nixon was grooming Elvis for the Presidency. (1984)

September

•

I don't need no bodyguard.
—Jimmy Hoffa

•

SEPTEMBER

1 After 155 days at sea, <u>Mobro</u>'s garbage is laid to rest: it's unloaded in Brooklyn. (1987)

2 A Hofmuseum professor decides the portfolio of the young man from Braunau is "good," but not good enough for entry to Vienna's Academy of Fine Arts; so Adolf Hitler seeks a new career path. (1910)

3 Under the command of E. Howard Hunt, the White House "plumbers" burglarize the office of Daniel Ellsberg's psychiatrist. The CIA helps out by providing Hunt with a red wig. (1971)

4 Tiny Tim marries Miss Vickie. (1972)

5 A woman "finds" an envelope full of money and, sure that it's "a gift from St. Jude," pays off all her debts, only to be arrested and charged with larceny. (1985) ☣

6 On this day a member of "the press" will ask of someone who has just won or lost a competition, or who is in shock or grief, "What was running through your mind when . . . "

7 A fifteen-year-old is crowned the first Miss America. (1921)

8 Roy Rogers' horse Trigger is dead, stuffed, and mounted. (1963) ☻

9 80,000 buttons with the slogan "Think Toy Safety," paid for and distributed by the United States Consumer Product Safety Commission, are recalled because they're dangerously sharp, coated with lead paint, and easy to swallow. (1970) ☣

10 First freeway opens. (1921)

SEPTEMBER

11 For the first time, the Miss America Pageant is televised coast-to-coast. (1954)

12 Counting down . . . 48 hours more . . . until "Entertainment Tonight" premieres. (1981)

13 Henry Bliss is run over and killed by a car in New York City and thus marks the nation's first death from an automobile accident. (1899)

14 The U.S. borrows its first money: $191,668.81 to pay the salaries of the President and Congress. (1789)

15 USA Today first graces the country's newsstands. (1982)

16 On his official visit to the United States, Soviet Premier Khrushchev's request for permission to visit Disneyland is denied on security grounds. (1959)

17 Twelve years after they were donated to the University of Maryland, the hundreds of boxes containing Spiro Agnew's papers remain unopened. (1985)

18 <u>The New York Times</u> begins publication. (1851)

19 Chicago Cubs owner Phil Wrigley shares his thoughts on baseball's first night game—"Just a passing fancy." (1935)

20 America's first shopping mall opens in Seattle. (1951)

21 Ex-Secretary of the Interior James Watt is appointed to the PTL board. (1982)

22 Donna Rice refuses to tell Barbara Walters whether or not she slept with Gary Hart "because it's a question of dignity." (1988)❷

23 "Our little girl—Tricia, the six-year-old—named it Checkers. And you know, the kids love the dog, and I just want to say this right now, that regardless of what they say about it, we're gonna keep it!" (1953)

24 Chicago Bears quarterback Jim Hardy is intercepted eight times; and it was only against the Eagles. (1950)

SEPTEMBER

25 Gary Hart's wife, Lee, shares her thoughts on the mess: "If I could have planned his weekend schedule, I think I would have scheduled it differently." (1987) ❷

26 Donald Trump completes his first deal. (1975) ❷

27 The Washington Senators change the course of history when they fail to call Fidel Castro back after his initial tryout. (1947)

28 Eight members of the Chicago White Sox are indicted for throwing the 1919 World Series to Cincinnati. (1920)

29 Birth of Bryant Gumbel. (1948)

30 Willard Scott stops and ponders life, and concludes that all in all, only good things happened yesterday. (1948)

October

•

Nobody now fears that a Japanese fleet
could deal an unexpected blow . . . radio
makes surprises impossible.
—Secretary of the Navy Josephus Daniels

•

OCTOBER

1 In 1926—after a life of courageous feats of derring-do, including twice over Niagara Falls—New Zealand's Bobby Leach fatally slips on an orange peel in Christchurch.

2 Stores are now decorated for The Holidays, and they've turned that music on.

3 1913: United States federal income tax is signed into law. 1917: Congress doubles the federal income tax rates.

4 America's second shopping mall opens in Framingham, Massachusetts. (1951)

5 The National Pork Producers Council announces it will no longer sponsor a National Pork Queen. (1987)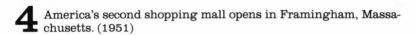

6 Mrs. O'Leary sets a lantern near her Guernsey and thinks nothing of it, whereas what little's left of Chicago 48 hours from now certainly will. (1871)

7 In the confusion after police pull over a speeding car in the nation's capital, Fanne Foxe jumps into the tidal basin, is fished out, and then returned to her companion—Wilbur Mills, House Ways and Means Committee Chairman. (1974)

8 Georgia Tech 222, Cumberland University 0. (1916)

9 Neiman-Marcus announces its "big gift" for the season—a $30,000 gold omelette pan. (1976)

10 Exactly what day in 1942 was the ultimate bad one for 39-year-old Harry Edsel Smith, we don't know, but his gravestone reads: "Looked up the elevator shaft to see if the car was on the way down. It was."

11 Thomas Carlyle's charwoman inadvertently burns his just finished manuscript of <u>The French Revolution</u>. So he sits down today to write it again. (1835)

12 Ted Turner explains why he's not selling the Atlanta Hawks even though the team's losing money: "My wife and children are liabilities, and I haven't sold them." (1983)❷

13 Charles Ford's book, which maintains that the world is flat, is doing very nicely at Scribner's Bookstore. (1932)

14 In Berkeley, poet Allen Ginsberg and Hell's Angels president Sonny Barger share some LSD in the evening, and by morning they're chanting together. (1965)

15 "Gone With the Wind" limited edition dinner plates on sale via TV's Home Shopping Network. (1988)

OCTOBER

16 Suzanne Sommers debuts. (1946)

17 Boardinghouse keepers in New York City band together and agree to serve boarders only four prunes each at breakfast. (1824)

18 Eddie Fisher's "Cindy, Oh, Cindy" released. (1956) ☣

19 Dow Jones Average drops 508 points. (1987)

20 Jacqueline Kennedy marries Aristotle Onassis. (1968)

21 It's three days since the Museum of Modern Art inadvertently hung Matisse's Le Bateau upside down and no one's yet noticed the mistake . . . and neither will any of the 100,000 viewers over the next 44 days. (1961)

22 Henry Kissinger still at large. (1989)

23 Tomorrow, and almost a year to the day from the big drop, General Motors stock closes down 50%. (1930)

24 Bert Parks will not emcee Miss America contest next year. (1979)

25 Using tourist maps to get around, the United States invades Grenada. (1983)

26 <u>The Harvard Economic Society Journal</u>, which just recently reported "end of the decline and revival for the remainder of the year," ceases publication due to lack of funds. (1931)

27 <u>Maltese Falcon</u> colorized. (1987)

28 Shere Hite's <u>Hite Report</u> on bestseller list . . . under non-fiction. (1977)

29 The New York Stock market crashes and the Great Depression begins. (1929)

30
Yesterday, 61 years after its development commenced, the first ballpoint pen is sold in America, and penmanship takes a turn for the worse. (1945)

31
"Pledge at least $100! Borrow it if necessary." —Reverend Ike (1968)

November

•

The French People are incapable
of regicide.

—Louis XVI

•

NOVEMBER

1 Rasputin meets the Russian Imperial family. (1905)

2 Dr. Richard J. Gatling patents the revolving 6-barrel machine gun. (1863)

3 Genghis Khan's birthday. (1167)

4 Millard Fillmore runs for President on the "Know-Nothing" ticket. (1856)

5 Chuck Colson declares that broadcaster "John Chancellor's performance is scandalous, yellow, shabby journalism" and that "we should break his goddamned nose." (1971)

6 "You won't have Dick Nixon to kick around anymore." (1962)

7 University of Oklahoma President, Dr. George L. Cross, declares, "We want to build a university our football team can be proud of." (1952) ☢

8 After consideration of 18,000 possibilities, the Ford Motor Executive Committee rejects them all and chooses instead to name their new car "Edsel." (1956)

9 800,000 are stranded inside New York City subways during the "great blackout" (1965); and Baltimore does it again, this time as the birthplace, in 1918, of Spiro Agnew.

10 First Women's Christian Temperance Union convention opens. (1891)

11 Pessimist discovers that "Genghis" Khan is now spelled "Jen-ghiz", which by itself is not much, but when you tally up all the other Chinese name changes . . .

12 Washington State and San Jose State play a football game and the total paid attendance is one. (1955)

13 The last "Li'l Abner" comic strip runs. (1977)

14 Vice-President Spiro Agnew declares that the millions of Americans demonstrating in their towns and cities against the Vietnam War are "encouraged by an effete corps of snobs who characterize themselves as intellectuals." (1969)

15 In a 1964 game against San Diego, Kansas City quarterback Len Dawson fumbles seven times.

16 The University of Nebraska expurgates seven pages of <u>Marketing Management: Text and Cases</u> because they contain a case study dealing with a firm that sells contraceptive devices. (1981)➣

17 A clerk in the Department of State successfully proposes that photographs be required as part of U.S. passports. (1912)

18 The United States population is now 200 million. (1967)

19 Nation's press touts Edward Everett's two hour speech and ignores President Lincoln's address at Gettysburg. (1863)

NOVEMBER

20 Michael Cimino's $44-million <u>Heaven's Gate</u> premieres. (1980)

21 Vanna White explains, "It's not the most intellectual job in the world, but I do have to know the letters." (1986) ♣

22 Cadillac introduces the 270-horsepower engine. (1954)

23 Johns Hopkins professor accuses Ptolemy of faking figures. (1954)

24 Louis Vuitton $275 knapsack doing very well in the stores. (1978)

25 Ivan Boesky: "I think greed is healthy." (1986)

26 Pat Robertson has to get married. (1957) ❷

27 After having been Christianized by Jean Carter Stapleton, Larry Flynt promises a new <u>Hustler</u> with a "healthy attitude toward sex mixed with a spiritual message." (1977)

NOVEMBER

28 The absolutely only copies—even including carbons—of many of Hemingway's short stories are stolen from Hadley's luggage at the Gare de Lyon. (1922)

29 Wallis (Warfield) Simpson meets the Prince of Wales/Duke of Windsor. (1930) ☣

30 Birth of Dick Clark. (1929)

December

•

I could not help being charmed by his
gentle, simple bearing, and his calm,
detached poise.
— Winston Churchill,
on Benito Mussolini

•

DECEMBER

1 Dr. Ruth's <u>First Love: A Young People's Guide to Sexual Information</u>, which mistakenly advises readers that the safest time to have sex is during a woman's most fertile period, is now being shipped to bookstores. (1984)

2 <u>USA Today</u> reports that 17% of all Americans would throw their pets off a cliff for $1 million. (1988) ➷

3 Rod McKuen publishes his first poem. (1960) ❷

4 Somebody, somewhere, will be forced to eat haggis today.

DECEMBER

5 Birth of Strom Thurmond. (1902)

6 New York's Metropolitan Museum of Art announces, 44 years after its acquisition, that its Greek bronze horse is a forgery. (1967)

7 The first one-way traffic regulation goes into effect (in New York City). (1791)

8 Before the day is out you will be ordered to have a nice day any number of depressing times.

9 Founding of John Birch Society. (1958)

10 "All of you who can give $100 come up to the front of the altar—no change please—hold those bills high, I want everyone to see your faith!"—Reverend Ike (1970)

DECEMBER

11 This is National Ding-a-Ling Day, which is sponsored by the National Ding-a-Ling Club to promote the concept that "just because a person is a ding-a-ling doesn't mean he or she can't be a wonderful, friendly, intelligent, loving, responsible and desirable person."

12 Birth of Frank Sinatra. (1915)

13 And on TV, in front of millions of viewers all across the country, still another Queen for a Day bares her embarrassments and tragedies for the pay-off—a new toaster. (1969)

14 Lee Iacocca's Chrysler pleads "no contest" to charges of tampering with the odometers of cars previously used for testing but sold as new. (1987)

DECEMBER

15 $32 million budgeted to make the film <u>Raising the Titanic</u>, three times what it cost to build the ship. (1986)

16 Gary Hart jumped back into the 1987 White House race yesterday, saying "let the people decide."

17 John DeLorean is found not guilty of embezzling $8.5 million. (1986)

18 Seasonal depression the topic of many newspaper and magazine articles.

19 Restoration experts today conclude that the discoloration near the base of the Statue of Liberty results from its patina being worn away by laborers urinating from the top of the statue. (1986)

20 In his quest to bring us culture as well as jugglers, Ed Sullivan introduces Salvador Dali on his stage to paint a picture with a water gun. (1967)

21 Birth of Kurt Waldheim. (1918)

22 Elvis Presley visited the White House yesterday to ask that President Nixon name him a "federal-agent-at-large working against the drug problem." (1970)

23 Last week the Coca-Cola Company boosted wholesale prices and today the 5-cent Coke is history. (1950)

24 God says to Pat Robertson, according to Pat Robertson, "Pat, I want you to have an RCA transmitter." (1986)

25 The last Christmas for Scribner's Bookstore in New York City. (1988)

26 European Parliament petitioned to outlaw Australian sport involving the throwing of dwarfs. (1985)

DECEMBER

27 A ballplayer, for the first time, sells, repeat, sells his autograph to an admiring child. (1986)

28 Miss Cheerleader U.S.A. competition opens in Cypress Gardens, Florida. (1969)

29 Time to start thinking about investing in next year's <u>Legs Diamond</u> revival.

30 In a year end wrap-up, <u>The New York Times</u> says that the U.S. has had a year of "wonderful prosperity." (1928)

31 Watch out, there's another damn new year coming!

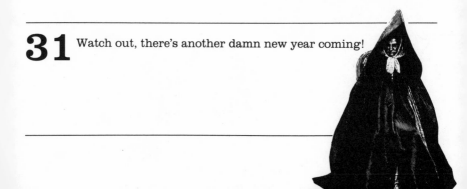

SHARE YOUR BAD DAYS
RECEIVE A FREE JOURNAL!
(Big Deal)

The authors solicit your very own bad days for any (Lord help us!) subsequent editions of THE PESSIMIST'S JOURNAL OF VERY, VERY BAD DAYS. Bad news travels fast but not far enough, so this is your chance to spread a little bad cheer.

Send your favorite Bad Day on a postcard with your name and address to: The Pessimist, Box 1950, Boston, MA 02130.

If we use your Bad Day, you'll be sent a copy of the next edition. We can't acknowledge the receipt of such submissions (what do you take us for, anyhow?). You'll have to trust us to be fair, as Ivan Boesky might have said. There will be duplicates, of course, so of each submission we use, the sender of the first received will be the one to get the book.

Have a nice day.

a pessimist
   production